Exquisite Embellishments for Paper Crafts™

Table of Contents

Fabulous Flowers

Paper Pretties

Pearls & Pins

Notable Naturals

Exquisite Embellishments 3
for Paper Crafts

{im·*be*·lish·**mənt**}

noun: a decorative detail or feature added to something to make it more attractive.

Keri Lee Sereika

Keri, currently living in South Carolina, is a stay at home mother of four and wife to a USAFR pilot. She has authored crafting articles for a variety of magazines and online media and has had her designs featured in numerous publications. When she's not busy playing with her kids, you'll find Keri in her studio creating projects or researching and writing articles on crafting.

The word embellishment as shown above is simply defined as an item that makes something more attractive. If I were to paraphrase and give my own definition of embellishment, as it pertains to paper crafting, I would say it is the item that makes the difference between a nice project and a beautiful or perfect project!

When it comes to embellishing a project my own personal style varies greatly depending on my mood. There are days where a smart, sharp flat-front knot is all I want. Those are the days I crave fresh and simple. Then there are days where I cannot seem to have enough layers and complexity! I find I have to add some glitter here, some ribbon there, a button with a bit of twine through the center, perhaps a swirl of pearls. Whether your personal taste is simplistic and clean or layered and complex, I believe this book will fit right in with your style.

If you are a novice paper crafter, you may find this book to be a treasure trove of delightful new ideas and inspirations. As a more seasoned paper crafter, these instructions may not be new, but perhaps they will remind you of ways to create using a long-forgotten embellishment technique. Our aim was to make the information appropriate for all levels of crafters, novice to seasoned designer alike. From a reader's standpoint we hope that you, the reader, walk away feeling educated, challenged and inspired. Our hope is that you feel you have been given good, solid instruction and education on how to not only use the embellishments you have on hand, but also to be inspired to try using them in different and unusual ways. We want you to feel challenged to think outside the box and rather than just tying the perfect bow and calling it complete, perhaps you will then accent the bow using an embellished button, an altered brad or a handmade, die-cut blossom. Our hope is that we will inspire the novice crafter to feel able to create the projects shown, as well as inspire the seasoned crafter to rethink what products to use when embellishing paper-crafted projects.

Embellishment Techniques

Buttons & Brads

Decorative Button Stickpin

1. Select a long stickpin and a button with a shank.

2. Thread stickpin through shank of button. Apply small amount of hot glue and allow it to cool completely.

3. Once cool, thread stickpin through center of knot on ribbon to showcase decorative button stickpin.

Embossed & Glittered Brad

Note: When embossing small items or metal items, make sure to use metal-tipped tweezers with coated handles, such as Precision Tweezers from We R Memory Keepers, to protect fingers from heat.

1. Hold brad using tweezers with coated handles. Use embossing heat tool to heat head of brad.

2. Dip head of brad into embossing powder. Reheat until embossing powder melts.

3. Repeat steps 1 and 2 until brad is fully embossed.

4. Add shine by dipping heated brad head into glitter while embossing powder is still hot.

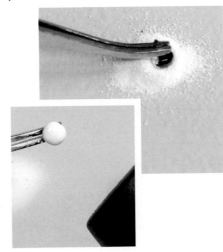

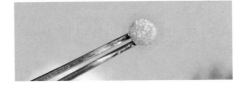

5. Heat one last time, very quickly, to set glitter in molten embossing powder to finish brad.

Backstitching

1. Use needle to pre-pierce stitch holes as needed.

2. Come up from bottom of panel through first hole; go down into second hole.

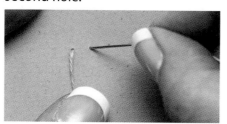

3. Pull thread taut to create first stitch.

4. Come up from bottom of panel through next hole and go back down into previous hole.

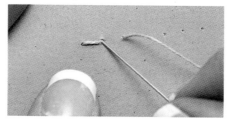

5. Repeat step 4 with each subsequent hole; retreat back down one hole to create line of stitches.

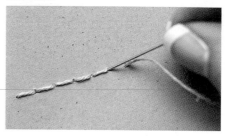

Cross-Stitching

1. Use needle to pre-pierce a double line of stitch holes. Come up from bottom of panel through first hole on bottom row.

2. Retreat down second hole on top row, creating a diagonal stitch.

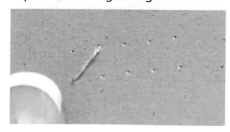

3. Come up from bottom of panel through first hole on top row. Retreat down second hole on bottom row to create "X" stitch.

4. Repeat steps, alternating starting at top or bottom so stitches stay tight.

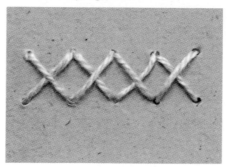

Blanket Stitching

1. Use needle to pre-pierce a line of holes approximately ¼ inch from edge of panel.

2. Come up from bottom of panel through bottom hole.

3. Retreat down second hole and come around from back of panel to thread needle through loop of first stitch before pulling thread taut.

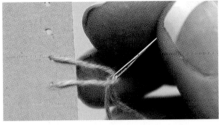

4. Retreat down third hole. Come around from back of panel to thread needle through loop of second stitch before pulling thread taut.

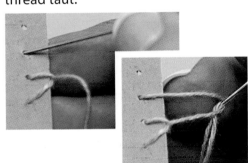

5. Repeat stitch until desired length of stitching is reached.

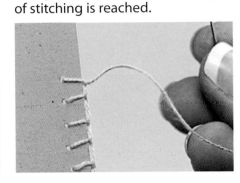

Securing Stitches on Back of Project

1. Place adhesive dot over threads at ends of stitching. Cut small pieces of scrap cardstock and press against adhesive dots to adhere.

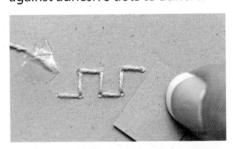

2. Snip ends of thread protruding from beneath cardstock scraps to keep panel neat and tidy. This is also a very helpful tip when machine stitching. Simply pull on bobbin thread to pull both threads through to bottom of panel, then apply adhesive dots and scrap of cardstock to hold stitches from pulling loose.

The Perfect Bow

1. Cross left ribbon (blue) over right ribbon (gold).

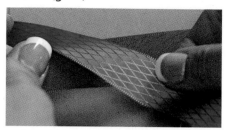

2. Pass blue ribbon under gold.

3. Pull both ribbons vertical to create finger-tight knot.

4. Fold gold ribbon into loop.

5. Wrap blue ribbon around back of gold loop to front right of gold loop.

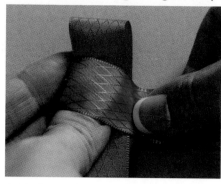

6. To form second loop, hold base of gold loop with one hand and use other hand to slide blue ribbon through gap underneath gold loop. Pull blue loop through to upper left corner of card.

7. Straighten loops and pull both tight slowly to keep front ribbon of bow flat and neat.

8. Complete a single-color bow; always finish bow by trimming tails to reduce effects of fraying.

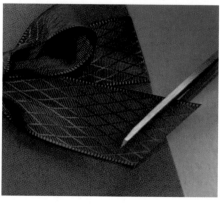

Flat-Front Knot

1. Begin by following steps 1–6 of The Perfect Bow instructions; pull loops all the way through and pull both ribbons tight slowly to keep front ribbon of knot flat and neat.

2. Trim tails at an angle for a quick and simple tailed knot.

3. To create a "V-notch" tail, simply fold ribbon tail in half lengthwise and cut from edges to fold, angling scissors toward knot.

4. Repeat step 3 for second side of knot.

Sewn Ruffled Ribbon

1. Using a sewing machine or hand-stitching, sew a long basting stitch down center of ribbon of your choice. ***Note:*** *If hand-stitching, make sure to knot end of thread before stitching.*

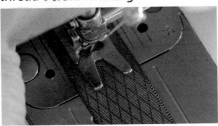

2. Sew entire length of ribbon and cut threads with 4 to 6 inches extra at end.

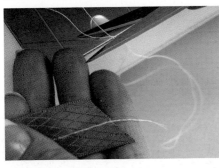

3. Pull on threads, causing ribbon to bunch.

4. Lay ribbon flat and move it along threads to create an even gather.

5. Apply a length of heavy-duty double-sided adhesive like Scor-Tape to project; remove tape backing.

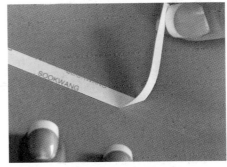

6. Press ruffled ribbon over adhesive strip on panel; press to fully adhere.

Non-Sewn Pleated Ribbon

1. Apply a length of heavy-duty double-sided adhesive like Scor-Tape to project.

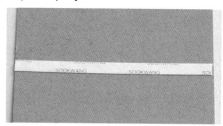

2. Remove tape backing; lay end of ribbon over edge of panel and press down. Begin to fold ribbon

back and forth to create a pleat, pressing ribbon into double-sided adhesive with fingers at each fold.

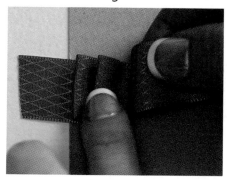

3. Once other edge is reached, finger-press each pleat to fully crease ribbon.

4. Trim ends and repress edges to be sure they are secure.

Heat-Scrunched Ribbon

1. Tie a bow onto project using organdy ribbon. Using a bamboo skewer, hold down tail of one side of bow. Pass a heat tool over top of ribbon in short small strokes to heat ribbon and melt it slightly. ***Note:*** *Be careful when heating ribbon as it takes only seconds to overheat and possibly burn the ribbon.*

2. Repeat on other ribbon tail as well as bow loops. Trim ribbon tails.

Colored Ribbon—Alchohol Marker Technique

1. Begin by placing a piece of waxed paper or other nonporous surface beneath ribbon.

2. Place flat edge of alcohol-based marker onto ribbon about 2 inches from end and draw marker down toward end of ribbon. Repeat as necessary until full coverage is achieved.

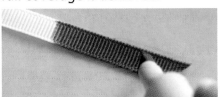

3. Hold colored end of ribbon down with index finger and spread fingers approximately 2½ inches apart. Begin coloring process, again drawing marker toward index finger.

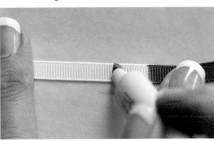

4. Repeat steps 2 and 3 until entire length of ribbon is colored to desired saturation. Let dry completely before applying to project.

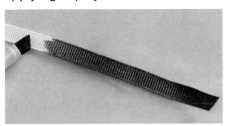

Colored Ribbon—Ink Pad Technique

1. Wrap thin strip of waxed paper around thumb of nondominant hand. Cut length of ribbon and place between thumb and dye ink pad of choice.

2. Press gently and pull ribbon through from between thumb and ink pad.

3. Pull ribbon through repeatedly until desired saturation is achieved. Allow ribbon to sit a moment for ink to dry fully before applying to project.

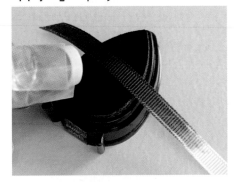

4. Remove waxed paper strip; take note of all the ink that is NOT on your thumb as well as the fact that there was no ink wasted by using a sponge to apply pressure to ribbon.

Fabulous Flowers

Rolled Ribbon Rose

Note: *If using hot glue to secure ribbon, be careful not to apply glue to fingers. If using quick-drying fabric glue, secure end of ribbon with straight pin until glue has dried as noted in instructions. Adjust fingers as needed to ensure a tight wrap.*

1. Cut a 24-inch length of ribbon. Twist 2 inches from end twice.

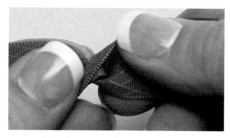

2. Holding 2-inch end of ribbon, bring long end (working end) of ribbon to the front over 2-inch tail and wrap around twist to create center of rose.

3. Twist working end of ribbon backwards and wrap around to front. In the same manner as before, twist working end of ribbon a second time before reaching starting point.

4. Repeat step 3.

5. Repeat step 3, applying a small dot of hot glue or quick-drying fabric adhesive to bottom edge of rose before wrapping.

6. Repeat step 5, folding, gluing and wrapping until desired size of rose is achieved. ***Note:*** *Reposition fingers as needed to ensure a tight wrap.* As flower grows larger in diameter, twist ribbon three or four times while wrapping around flower's center as desired.

7. Once rose is desired size, if using fast-drying fabric glue, secure working end with a straight pin by running straight pin through flower. Trim 2 inches at an angle to approximately 1 inch and adhere to bottom of flower. Secure with straight pin if needed while glue dries.

8. In the same manner as before, remove straight pin, if used, and wrap working end of ribbon around flower one last time. Trim at an angle and adhere to outside edge of flower. If using fast-drying fabric glue, secure with straight pins as needed while glue dries. Trim ends as needed after completely dry and adhere to project.

Felt-Loop Fringe Flower

1. Fold a 1 x 12-inch length of wool felt in half lengthwise. Cut a circle of felt approximately 1 inch across.

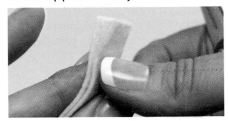

2. Hold fold facing dominant hand and snip ⅜-inch-long cuts from folded edge toward free edges approximately ¼ inch apart.

3. Begin to roll folded, cut felt from one end.

4. Continue to roll, holding tight to center of flower from both top and bottom.

5. As you continue to roll, apply light pressure to outer edge of flower to create a widening base. This will give the flower both width as well as keep it flatter rather than puffier.

6. Once you reach the end of the length, adhere end using a dot of hot glue. Apply hot glue to spiral on back side of flower.

7. Cover hot glue with felt circle; press and hold until glue cools.

8. Use fingers to fluff flower from top side prior to attaching to project.

Paper Pretties
Create a Tag

1. Use sharp paper snips to cut off right corner of rectangular-shaped panel.

2. Using cut-off corner as a template, trace along longest edge with a pencil.

3. Cut along pencil line.

4. Use hole punch to punch hole in center between cut-off corners.

5. Tie finished tag to project by threading twine or ribbon through hole.

6. To create a banner end tag, use ruler and pencil to mark center of bottom of tag approximately ½ inch above bottom edge.

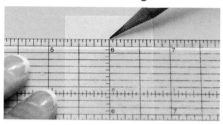

7. Cut from left corner to center mark.

8. Cut from right corner to center mark to complete banner end.

3-D Cardstock Star

1. Beginning with die-cut or punched star, use bone folder and foam mat to score lines from tip of star to just short of center of star.

2. Repeat with remaining points of star. Turn star over.

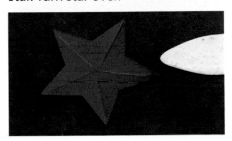

3. Gently pinch along scored lines to create depth.

4. Use dye ink and sponge daubers to ink edges of star to accentuate depth.

5. Apply ink to scored lines along top of star to finish 3-D effect and adhere to card front.

Pleated Cardstock Strip

1. Cut a 1 x 12-inch piece of cardstock. Pull cardstock between thumb and bone folder to gently break down fibers of cardstock, making strip pliable.

2. Don't be concerned if paper curls; simply flip strip over and repeat on opposite side, pulling gently between thumb and bone folder until cardstock strip is soft and pliable.

3. Apply a length of heavy-duty double-sided adhesive like Scor-Tape to project. Remove tape backing; lay end cardstock at edge of panel and press down. Begin to fold cardstock back and forth to create a pleat, pressing with fingers at each fold.

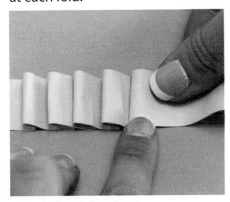

4. Tie a length of ribbon around top edge of pleated strip to create a wonderful 3-D paper embellishment.

Pearls & Pins

Pearls & Pins
Colored Pearls

1. Begin with white, cream or very pale colored self-adhesive pearls and a mid-range color alcohol marker. Apply a layer of color onto pearl. Allow to dry.

2. Reapply additional layers of color until desired color saturation is achieved.

3. Allow pearls a moment to dry before applying to project.

Decorative Stickpin

1. Choose a variety of coordinating beads and a pearl-topped stickpin.

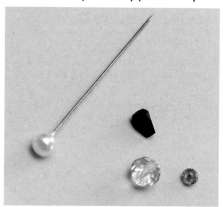

2. Thread beads onto pin.

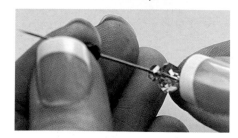

3. Add a small drop of super glue to final bead. Hold pin at angle until glue dries.

4. Embellish project with finished stickpin as desired.

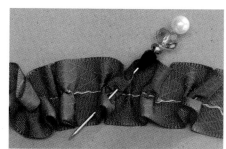

Buttons & Brads

Embellishing a project with the perfect ribbon and bow doesn't mean the project is complete. Taking the embellishment factor from finished to fabulous can happen easily by adding a simple selection of buttons or brads. Not having "just the right" button or brad on hand can be very frustrating; knowing how to alter those items is priceless. Boasting a variety of uses, both buttons and brads are an inexpensive and fun way to dress up the corners of a stamped panel, the center of a bow or flower, a layered die cut and more.

Vintage Card

Design by **Kandis Smith**

Form a 4¼ x 5½-inch card from cardstock.

Referring to photo, cut six 5¼-inch-long strips from various printed papers in desired widths. Adhere to card front. Stamp sentiment onto card front as shown. Zigzag-stitch along long edges of paper strips.

Cut ends of twill ribbon into V-notches and adhere horizontally to card front. Attach corrugated heart over twill ribbon using foam tape.

Thread button with baker's twine; tie bow on front and trim ends. Attach button to corrugated heart using adhesive dots. ❧

Sources: *Printed papers from Crate Paper Inc.; corrugated heart from Jillibean Soup; stamp set from Hero Arts; adhesive dots from Glue Dots; paper adhesive from Tombow USA.*

Materials

- Kraft cardstock
- Emma's Shoppe Collection printed papers
- Kraft corrugated heart
- Thank You For Being My Friend stamp set
- Black dye ink pad
- Green/white baker's twine
- Red button
- 4⅝ inches ¾-inch-wide yellow twill ribbon
- Sewing machine
- Brown thread
- Adhesive foam tape
- Adhesive dots
- Paper adhesive

Button Heart

Design by **Melissa Phillips**

Form a 2⅞ x 5¼-inch card from cardstock. Using paintbrush, lightly brush paint onto edges of card front. Let dry.

Cut a 2½ x 4¾-inch piece from cream printed paper; ink edges light brown. Adhere to card front. Using pinking shears, cut two 2½ x 1¼-inch fabric pieces, one from floral fabric and one from blue plaid fabric. Adhere to card front as shown.

Machine-stitch around fabric and printed paper panels as desired.

Using black ink, stamp button heart and sentiment onto card front. Color image with markers.

Thread buttons with string. Adhere buttons to button heart image as desired. Cut two small flowers from crochet trim; adhere to button heart. Attach pearls to centers of crochet flowers. Apply glitter glue to remaining buttons on stamped image; let dry.

Cut ribbon into a 5-inch length and a 5½-inch length. Secure end of shorter length of ribbon to card back. Secure one end of longer length of ribbon inside card. Bring remaining ends of ribbon to front of card; tie a bow and trim ends.

Adhere paper flower to bow. ❧

Sources: Cardstock and stamp set from Papertrey Ink; fabric from United Notions/Moda Fabrics; Button Heart stamp from Red Lead Paperworks; markers from Imagination International Inc.; paper flower from Prima Marketing Inc.; glitter glue from Ranger Industries Inc.; fabric glue from Beacon Adhesives Inc.

Materials

- Pink cardstock
- Life's Journey Paper Collection
- Cream printed paper
- Fabric: cream floral, blue plaid
- Stamps: Button Heart, Peaceful Garden set
- Dye ink pads: light brown, black
- Antique white acrylic paint
- Copic® markers: G12, YG91
- 10½ inches ½-inch-wide cream twill ribbon
- 1 small white paper flower
- Light tan floral crochet trim
- White string
- 2 light green self-adhesive pearls
- Assorted cream/white buttons
- Paintbrush
- Pinking shears
- Sewing machine
- Light green thread
- Iridescent glitter glue
- Fabric glue
- Paper adhesive

Materials

- Pink cardstock
- Bubblegum Hills 6 x 6 paper pad
- Fillable Frames #4 stamp set
- Dark brown dye ink pad
- Miscellaneous pastel-colored buttons
- Pink star stickpin
- White/lime green baker's twine
- Fabric glue
- Quick-drying paper adhesive

Happy Birthday Buttons

Design by **Sherry Wright**

Form a 5½ x 5½-inch card from cardstock.

Cut a 5½ x 5½-inch piece from green printed paper and a 5 x 5-inch piece from polka-dot printed paper. Layer and adhere to card front as shown.

Cut a 4 x 4-inch piece from pink printed paper; ink edges dark brown. Adhere to card front.

Cut a 3 x 2¼-inch piece from blue printed paper. Referring to photo, trim edges at an angle to create a cupcake wrapper. Ink edges dark brown. Adhere to card front.

Referring to photo and using fabric glue, arrange and adhere buttons to card, creating the top of the cupcake.

Adhere a piece of baker's twine along top edge of cupcake wrapper. Tie a bow with baker's twine; trim long ends and adhere to cupcake wrapper. Secure ends of bow to card front as shown.

Cut a 5 x ¾-inch strip from blue printed paper; cut a V-notch at each end. Stamp sentiment onto strip; ink edges dark brown. Fold sentiment strip in half and wrap around stickpin as shown; adhere in place. Slide stickpin behind buttons; adhere as needed. ❧

Sources: *Cardstock from Bazzill Basics Paper Inc.; paper pad from Kaisercraft; stamp set from Papertrey Ink; fabric glue and quick-drying paper adhesive from Beacon Adhesives Inc.*

Glittered Butterfly

Design by **Teresa Kline**

Form a 4¼ x 5½-inch card from cardstock.

Adhere a 4¼ x 5½-inch piece of Happy Polka Dots paper and a 4¼ x 2-inch piece of blue scroll paper together as shown, creating a 4¼ x 5½-inch panel.

Cut doily in half and adhere to paper panel as shown. Adhere lace to panel, covering top edge of doily.

Apply double-sided tape to panel where ribbon will be attached. Referring to photo, gather ribbon along length of tape, pressing ribbon in place to secure. Wrap and adhere ends to back. Adhere to card front.

Using Beautiful Butterflies die set, die-cut a small butterfly from blue scroll paper and a large butterfly from cardstock. Apply clear-drying adhesive to front of each butterfly. Sprinkle with glitter. **Note:** *Gently press glitter into adhesive.* Layer and attach butterflies to card front as shown using foam tape; use double layers of foam tape as desired.

Stamp sentiment onto cardstock. Trim sentiment down to a 3 x ½-inch piece; cut right end into a V-notch. Curve sentiment piece using fingers and adhere to card front as shown. Do not apply adhesive to V-notched end.

Thread twine through button; tie bow on front and trim ends. Adhere to butterfly as shown. ✍

Sources: *Cardstock from Papertrey Ink; Happy Polka Dots printed paper from My Mind's Eye; stamp set from Verve Stamps; chunky glass glitter from Art Institute Glitter Inc.; button from Crate Paper Inc.; die set and clear-drying adhesive from Stampin' Up!; double-sided tape from Scor-Pal Products.*

Materials

- Cream cardstock
- Printed papers: Stella & Rose Hattie Happy Polka Dots, blue scroll
- 4-inch white paper doily
- Sunny Days Stamp Set
- Dark brown ink pad
- Clear chunky glass glitter
- 6 inches ½-inch-wide cream lace
- 12 inches ½-inch-wide brown ribbon
- Natural twine
- Portrait Eclectic Buttons: brown flower
- Beautiful Butterflies die set (#114507)
- Die-cutting machine
- Adhesive foam tape
- Double-sided tape
- Clear-drying paper adhesive

Reminiscing

Design by **Linda Lucas**

Project note: *Ink edges of all cut pieces dark brown, including card front.*

Form a 5¾ x 4¼-inch card from white cardstock. Adhere a 5⅝ x 4-inch piece of printed paper to card front.

Cut a 5½ x 4-inch piece from corrugated cardboard; tear off bottom and right edges. Ink front of cardboard dark brown.

Using black ink, stamp truck image onto white cardstock. Color image using foam dauber and desired colors of distress ink. Punch left edge using edger punch. Adhere to cardboard panel.

Wrap jute around layered image panel twice; secure ends to back. Adhere to card front.

Die-cut a 1⅝-inch sprocket from brown cardstock. In the same manner, die-cut a 1-inch sprocket from brown cardstock. Layer and adhere sprockets to card front as shown, using foam tape as desired.

Rough up front of button with sandpaper. Apply watermark ink to button and sprinkle with embossing powder; heat-emboss. Thread gold cord through buttonholes; tie knot on front and trim ends. Adhere to layered sprockets on card front. ✄

Sources: *Stamp from Darkroom Door; distress ink pads from Ranger Industries Inc.; watermark ink pad from Imagine Crafts/Tsukineko; embossing powder from Stampin' Up!; Edger Punch from EK Success; die templates from Spellbinders™ Paper Arts; double-sided tape from Imagination International Inc.*

Materials

- Cardstock: white, brown
- Corrugated cardboard
- Street map printed paper
- Old Truck photo stamp
- Distress ink pads: cream, dark brown, brown, green
- Black dye ink pad
- Watermark ink pad
- Gold embossing powder
- Natural jute
- Gold cord
- Wooden button
- Binding Edge Edger Punch
- Sprightly Sprockets die templates (#S5-048)
- Die-cutting machine
- Embossing heat tool
- Foam dauber
- Sandpaper
- Adhesive foam tape
- Double-sided tape

A Stitch in Time

Hey, Gnomie!

Sewing is an art of days gone by. Learning to bring the elements of thread and design into any project helps keep that art alive and adds interest and depth of texture. From hand-stitching to machine-stitching to faux-stitching, each stitch lends itself to developing the character and charm of the completed creation.

Head in the Clouds

Design by **Keri Lee Sereika**

Form a 5½ x 5½-inch card from olive green cardstock.

Cut a 5¼ x 5¼-inch piece from Chevron paper. Cut a 5¼ x ¾-inch piece from Chevron paper and a 5¼ x ½-inch piece from Galaxy paper. Layer and adhere printed paper pieces to Chevron panel as shown. Referring to photo, zigzag-stitch along top and bottom edges of paper pieces.

Wrap ribbon around panel as shown. Tie bow on right side; trim ends. Adhere to card front.

Stamp bunny in plane image onto a 4¼ x 3¼-inch piece of white smooth cardstock with black ink. Color using markers. Sponge blue ink onto top edge of panel.

Use a sewing needle to pierce holes behind airplane image as shown. Hand-stitch white thread through pierced holes. Tape ends of thread to back of panel. Adhere to light blue cardstock; trim a small border. Embellish with gems as shown. Attach to card front using foam squares.

Hand-cut a ⅜-inch circle from light blue cardstock; set aside. Cut a 6 x ½-inch strip from Chevron paper. Place strip onto scoring board with long edge horizontal. Score vertical lines every ¼ inch. Accordion-fold strip along scored lines. Adhere short ends of folded strip together. Press piece down creating a small medallion. Attach to hand-cut circle using adhesive dot. Attach to bow on card in the same manner.

Thread button with baker's twine and tie a triple bow on back side; trim ends. Attach to paper medallion using adhesive dots.

Stamp sentiment onto white smooth cardstock with black ink. Using 1⅜ x 1¾-inch Labels Eighteen die template, die-cut a label around sentiment; leave die template in place. Using airbrush system and B00 marker, color label; remove die template. Attach to card front as shown using foam squares. ✄

Sources: Printed papers from My Mind's Eye; stamp set from The Cat's Pajamas; dye ink pads from Imagine Crafts/Tsukineko; markers and airbrush system from Imagination International Inc.; baker's twine from The Twinery; self-adhesive gems from Queen & Co.; die templates and die-cutting machine from Spellbinders™ Paper Arts; scoring board and tool from Scor-Pal Products; foam squares from SCRAPBOOK ADHESIVES BY 3L™; adhesive dots from Therm O Web Inc.; quick-drying paper adhesive from Beacon Adhesives Inc.

Materials

- Cardstock: olive green, white smooth, light blue
- Lime Twist Out of the Blue printed papers: Family Chevron, Playful Galaxy
- Take Off stamp set (#K-1734 CL)
- Dye ink pads: black, blue
- Copic® markers: B00, B0000, BG10, R11, R39, T1, T3, W1
- 19½ inches ⅜-inch-wide cream twill ribbon
- Light blue/white baker's twine
- Brown button
- Cream thread
- 4 red self-adhesive gems
- Labels Eighteen die templates (#S4-310)
- Die-cutting machine
- Marker airbrush system
- Sewing needle
- Craft sponge
- Scoring board and tool
- Sewing machine with white thread
- Adhesive foam squares
- Adhesive dots
- Tape
- Quick-drying paper adhesive

Materials

- Cardstock: white smooth, brown, light brown, orange
- Emma's Shoppe printed papers: Fabric, Sweets, Books
- Fall Time Cocoa stamp set
- Black fine-detail dye ink pad
- Copic® markers: BG10, E31, E33, E35, R01, R11, Y19, YG03, YG05, YR04, YR09, YR16
- Colorless Blender (0)
- 11 inches ½-inch-wide brown/white dot ribbon
- 6 inches ⅝-inch-wide cream lace
- Baker's twine: orange/white, brown/white
- ⅛-inch hole punch
- Die templates: Labels Thirteen (#S4-248), Standard Circles SM (#S4-116), Standard Circles LG (#S4-114)
- Die-cutting machine
- Sewing machine with white thread
- Adhesive foam dots
- Double-sided adhesive
- Paper adhesive

Thankful for You

Design by **Jessica Fick**

Form a 4¼ x 5½-inch card from brown cardstock.

Cut a 4 x 5⅜-inch piece from light brown cardstock. Cut strips from printed papers. Adhere paper strips to light brown panel. Zigzag-stitch along top and bottom edges of paper strips.

Wrap lace around light brown panel; secure ends to back. Wrap orange/white baker's twine around lace three times; secure ends to back of panel.

Wrap ribbon around light brown panel as shown. Tie knot and trim ends. Adhere panel to card front.

Stamp sentiment onto light brown cardstock. Die-cut a 1⅝ x 1⅜-inch label around sentiment. Punch hole through top of sentiment label; thread brown/white baker's twine through hole and around knotted ribbon and tie bow. Trim ends. Secure as needed using double-sided adhesive.

Stamp image onto white smooth cardstock. Color using markers and Colorless Blender. Die-cut a 2¾-inch Standard Circles LG circle around image. Die-cut a 3-inch Standard Circles SM circle from orange cardstock. Layer and adhere circles together. Zigzag-stitch along edge of image circle. Attach to card front using foam dots. 🐭

Sources: *White smooth cardstock, markers and Colorless Blender from Imagination International Inc.; remaining cardstock from Stampin' Up!; printed papers from Crate Paper Inc.; stamp set from Sweet 'n Sassy Stamps; fine-detail ink pad from Imagine Crafts/Tsukineko; die templates from Spellbinders™ Paper Arts; foam dots from Plaid Enterprises Inc.; double-sided adhesive and paper adhesive from Tombow USA.*

Gnomie

Design by **Lori Craig**

Form a 4¼ x 5½-inch card from kraft cardstock.

Cut a 4¼ x 5½-inch piece from red cardstock. Referring to photo, adhere a 4 x 3¾-inch piece of Summer Fun paper to red panel. Machine-stitch a wavy line along edges of printed paper.

Cut a 6-inch piece from brown crepe paper. Referring to photo, gather and adhere crepe paper to red panel.

Adhere a 4¼ x ¾-inch piece of Summer Fun paper to red panel as shown. Machine-stitch along top and bottom edges of paper strip. Adhere red panel to card front.

Using Well Worn Greetings die set, cut a decorative shape from red cardstock and a slightly smaller decorative shape from Simple Pleasures paper. Using foam tape, layer and attach shapes to card front.

Stamp gnome onto white smooth cardstock. Color using markers. Cut out and attach to card front as shown using foam tape.

Cut a 3⅝ x 1-inch piece from kraft cardstock; cut a V-notch at each end. Ink edges white. Stamp sentiment onto right side of kraft piece with red ink. Using foam tape as desired, layer and attach paper flowers and sentiment panel to card front.

Color a piece of twine using desired marker; let dry. Thread twine through button; tie bow on front and trim ends. Attach to paper flower as shown. ✎

Sources: *White smooth cardstock, markers and double-sided adhesive from Imagination International Inc.; remaining cardstock from Stampin' Up!; printed papers from Simple Stories; stamp set from Gina K. Designs; pigment ink pad from Clearsnap Inc.; die set from My Favorite Things.*

Materials

- Cardstock: white smooth, kraft, red
- 100 Days of Summer printed papers: 100% Summer Fun, Simple Pleasures
- Brown crepe paper
- Gnome One Like You stamp set (#TMA-19)
- Ink pads: black dye, red dye, white pigment
- Copic® markers: BG11, BG15, E00, R22, R24, Y32
- Cream twine
- Yellow button
- White paper flowers: 1 medium, 1 large
- Well Worn Greeting die set
- Die-cutting machine
- Sewing machine
- White thread
- Adhesive foam tape
- Double-sided adhesive

Butterflies Gift Bag

Design by **Keri Lee Sereika**

Referring to photo throughout, adhere a piece of blue printed paper and a piece of pink printed paper to front of gift bag.

Die-cut three different Mini Exotic Butterflies from three different pieces of printed paper. Adhere butterflies to a piece of light blue cardstock as shown.

Place light blue panel on foam pad. Referring to photo, use paper piercer to pierce a curved line of holes below each butterfly. Connect lines using glitter pen. Adhere panel to bag as shown.

Cut a 21-inch length from seam binding and ruffle using sewing machine. Adhere to bag as shown.

Embellish bag with pearls.

Create a 2½ x 1¼-inch tag from light pink cardstock. Stamp sentiment onto tag. Punch a ⅛-inch hole through top of tag. Thread twine through hole and around bag handle; tie knot and trim ends.

Tie a double bow around bag handle with remaining length of seam binding. Trim ends. Attach gem to center of bow. 🦋

Sources: *Paper pad from My Mind's Eye; stamp set and dies from The Cat's Pajamas; glitter pen from Imagination International Inc.; self-adhesive pearls and gems from Queen & Co.; hole punch from Fiskars; quick-drying paper adhesive from Beacon Adhesives Inc.*

Materials

- Kraft gift bag
- Cardstock: light blue, light pink
- Stella Rose Hazel paper pad
- Bearing Flowers stamp set (#K-1737 CL)
- Black dye ink pad
- Silver glitter pen
- 40 inches ⅝-inch-wide gray seam binding
- Twine
- 4 large white self-adhesive pearls
- Pink large self-adhesive gem
- ⅛-inch hole punch
- Mini Exotic Butterflies dies (#DL112)
- Die-cutting machine
- Sewing machine
- Light gray thread
- Paper piercer
- Foam pad
- Quick-drying paper adhesive

JUST for You

Much Love

Design by **Nina Brackett**

Form a 4¼ x 5½-inch card from aqua cardstock.

Cut a 4¼ x 3½-inch piece from red text paper and a 4¼ x 1¾-inch piece from aqua/white dot paper. Adhere printed paper pieces to card front as shown. Zigzag-stitch along top and bottom edges.

Adhere doily to card front as shown.

Wrap seam binding around card front. Tie a multiple loop bow; trim ends.

Thread button with twine. Wrap twine around bow and tie a large bow; trim ends.

Using three different sized Classic Hearts die templates, cut three hearts from a variety of printed papers. Layer hearts together; machine-stitch down center of hearts. Adhere to card front. Adhere paper rose to center of layered hearts.

Stamp sentiment and banner onto white cardstock with black ink. Using corresponding Ribbon Banners die template, cut around sentiment banner. Ink edges light brown. Attach to card front as shown using foam tape. ✎

Sources: Cardstock from Papertrey Ink; Mini Deck from Cosmo Cricket; stamp set from Layers of Color; die templates and die-cutting machine from Spellbinders™ Paper Arts; foam tape from 3M; double-sided tape from Scor-Pal Products.

Materials

- Cardstock: aqua, white
- Odds & Ends Mini Deck
- White paper doily
- Sentimental Banners stamp set
- Dye ink pads: black, light brown
- 23 inches ⅝-inch-wide red seam binding
- White twine
- Red paper rose
- White button
- Die templates: Classic Hearts (#S4-136), Ribbon Banners (#S4-324)
- Die-cutting machine
- Sewing machine
- White thread
- Adhesive foam tape
- Double-sided tape

Rules for Ribbon

There is something about adding a piece of ribbon to any project that makes even the most appealing project more beautiful or more complete. Knowing how to best utilize ribbon is key to making the most of the ribbon chosen for each project. Whether it is being tied in the perfect bow or flat-front knot, altered using color or heat or ruffled, folded or rolled to form a flower, ribbon is one key ingredient that can be used in a variety of ways to create the perfectly finished project.

Blessings

Design by **Nina Brackett**

Form a 4¼ x 5½-inch card from kraft cardstock.

Cut two 4¼ x 2½-inch pieces from coordinating pieces of printed paper. Adhere to card front as shown, creating a 4¼ x 5-inch printed paper panel. Zigzag-stitch along top and bottom edges of printed paper panel.

Die-cut a 4¼-inch Parisian Accents border from white cardstock. Adhere to card front as shown.

Stamp floral heart onto white cardstock; color using markers, cut out. Attach to card front using foam tape.

Stamp "blessings" onto white cardstock; cut out. Adhere to card front as shown.

Wrap ribbon around card front as shown. Tie a multiple-loop bow; trim ends. Attach paper flower to bow using adhesive dot. 🐚

Sources: Cardstock from Gina K. Designs; Life's Journey Paper Collection from K&Company; stamp sets from Layers of Color; ink pad from Imagine Crafts/Tsukineko; markers from Imagination International Inc.; paper flower from Prima Marketing Inc.; die templates and die-cutting machine from Spellbinders™ Paper Arts; foam tape from 3M; double-sided tape from Scor-Pal Products.

Materials

- Cardstock: kraft, white
- Life's Journey Paper Collection
- Stamp sets: Renaissance Hearts, Artful Endearments
- Brown dye ink pad
- Copic® markers: BG10, BG11, BG13
- 30 inches ½-inch-wide white twill
- Light blue paper flower
- Parisian Accents die templates (#S5-034)
- Die-cutting machine
- Sewing machine
- White thread
- Adhesive foam tape
- Double-sided tape

Wonderful Friend

Design by **Heidi Blankenship**

Form a 5½ x 5½-inch card from tan cardstock. Adhere a 5¼ x 5¼-inch piece of brown cardstock to card front.

Cut a 5 x 5-inch piece from floral paper. Cut ribbon into four 2¾-inch lengths. Wrap a length of ribbon around a corner of floral panel; secure ends to back using tape. Repeat with remaining lengths of ribbon and corners of panel. Adhere to card front.

Stamp sentiment onto chipboard tag. Attach corresponding self-adhesive pearl design to tag. Attach to card front using foam dots.

Embellish card with pearls as shown. ❧

Sources: Printed paper from Pink Paislee; Nestaboard chipboard and self-adhesive pearls from Want2Scrap; stamp set from JustRite; ink pad from Imagine Crafts/Tsukineko; ribbon from Really Reasonable Ribbon; foam dots and paper adhesive from SCRAPBOOK ADHESIVES BY 3L™.

Materials

- Cardstock: tan, brown
- Butterfly Garden Collection Flower Blooms printed paper
- Nestaboard Fancy Tags Two chipboard
- You Inspire Me stamp set
- Brown dye ink pad
- 11 inches ⅝-inch-wide light brown satin ribbon
- White self-adhesive pearls: Nestabling Fancy Tags Two, 6 large, 2 small
- Tape
- Adhesive foam dots
- Paper adhesive

Bright Birthday Wishes

Design by **Tami Mayberry**

Form a 4¼ x 5½-inch card from orange cardstock.

Cut a 4¼ x 2¾-inch piece from red cardstock and a 4¼ x 2½-inch piece from printed paper. Layer and adhere to card front as shown.

Cut a 4¼ x 1¾-inch piece from orange cardstock, a 4¼ x 1½-inch piece from blue cardstock and a 4¼ x 1¼-inch piece from lime green cardstock. Layer and adhere cardstock pieces to card front as shown.

Stamp frame and sentiment onto red cardstock; cut out frame. Attach to card front as shown using foam tape.

Color small gems with markers; let dry. Attach to card front next to sentiment frame.

Color ribbon using blue marker; let dry. Wrap around top of card front; tie bow and trim ends.

Sources: *Printed paper from My Mind's Eye; stamp set from Gina K. Designs; markers from ShinHan USA Inc.; self-adhesive gems from Want2Scrap; ribbon from May Arts.*

Materials

- Cardstock: orange, red, blue, lime green
- Lime Twist Fly A Kite Genuine Bingo printed paper
- All Occasion Tags stamp set
- Black dye ink pad
- Alcohol markers: B63, GY48, R4, YR23
- 4 small clear self-adhesive gems
- 16½ inches ½-inch-wide white ribbon
- Adhesive foam squares
- Paper adhesive

Primitive Pumpkins

Design by **Teresa Kline**

Form a 4¼ x 5½-inch card from kraft cardstock.

Cut a 3¾ x 5-inch piece from Creepy Celebration paper and a 3¾ x 1½-inch piece from Happy Halloween paper. Adhere together as shown, creating a panel.

Stamp sentiment onto lower right corner of panel.

Using sewing machine, create a ruffled ribbon. Referring to photo, adhere ribbon to panel, securing ends to back. **Note:** *Apply adhesive along top and bottom of ribbon as needed to secure gathers.*

Machine-stitch along center of gathered ribbon. Zigzag-stitch along bottom edge of panel. Adhere to card front.

Stamp two pumpkins onto orange cardstock. Sprinkle with embossing powder; heat-emboss, cut out.

Using Houndstooth embossing folder, emboss pumpkins. Apply glitter glue to pumpkins as desired; let dry. Attach large pumpkin to card front using one layer of foam squares. Attach small pumpkin to card using two layers of foam squares.

Decorate inside of card as desired. ✈

Sources: *Cardstock from Papertrey Ink; printed papers from My Mind's Eye; stamp set from Verve Stamps; dye ink pad from Imagine Crafts/Tsukineko; ribbon from Stampin' Up!; double-sided tape from Scor-Pal Products.*

Materials

- Cardstock: kraft, orange
- Mischievous printed papers: Creepy Celebration, Happy Halloween
- Bountiful Harvest stamp set
- Black dye ink pad
- Black embossing powder
- 16 inches 1¼-inch-wide black/white striped ribbon
- Houndstooth embossing folder (#37-1167)
- Embossing machine
- Sewing machine
- Black thread
- Embossing heat tool
- Silver glitter glue
- Adhesive foam squares
- Double-sided tape
- Paper adhesive

Welcome Baby

Design by **Sharon M. Reinhart**

Form a 4¼ x 4¼-inch card from printed paper. Adhere a 3¾ x 3¾-inch piece of white cardstock to card front as shown.

Using 3½ x 3½-inch and 2 x 2-inch Classic Square LG die templates, cut a square frame from pink pearlescent cardstock.

In the same manner, cut and emboss a lacey frame from white cardstock using 3¼ x 3¼-inch Lacey Squares die template and 2 x 2-inch Classic Squares LG die template. Adhere white frame to pink frame.

Copy iris-folding pattern and attach faceup to work surface. Place layered frame facedown on top of iris-folding pattern; secure in place with removable tape.

Cut each length of ribbon into ten 3½-inch lengths. Referring to photo throughout, position one length of white ribbon on lower right corner of iris-folding pattern. Align edge of ribbon with line on pattern; secure one end of ribbon to back of frame with cellophane tape; trim excess and adhere opposite end of ribbon. **Note:** *This side is the back of the frame.* Repeat with pink ribbon on upper right corner followed by white ribbon in upper left corner and pink ribbon in lower left corner. Continue working around pattern counterclockwise until all areas are filled except for center square.

Cut a 2½ x 2½-inch piece from printed paper; adhere to center of iris-folding pattern, using double-sided tape on edges of square. Carefully remove frame from iris-folding pattern and turn faceup. Adhere to card front with foam tape.

Thread button with remaining length of desired color ribbon. Knot on front; trim ends. Adhere to card front as shown.

Attach gems to edges of frame.

Stamp "Welcome Baby" onto white cardstock. Punch out sentiment using 1-inch circle punch. Apply glitter glue to edges of circle. Let dry. Attach to card front using foam tape.

Decorate inside of card as desired. ❧

Sources: White cardstock from Bazzill Basic Papers Inc.; remaining cardstock from Paper and More!; printed paper from Bo-Bunny Press; stamp set from Stampin' Up!; pigment ink pad from Imagine Crafts/Tsukineko; ribbons from May Arts; die templates from Spellbinders™ Paper Arts; die-cutting and embossing machine from Sizzix; glitter glue from Ranger Industries Inc.; foam tape from 3M.

Materials

- Cardstock: white, pink pearlescent
- Passion Fruit Flourish printed paper
- Petite Pairs stamp set
- Pink pearlescent pigment ink pad
- 38 inches ⅜-inch-wide ribbon: pink dot, white/pink heart
- Cream button
- 6 pink self-adhesive gems
- 1-inch circle punch
- Die templates: Lacey Squares (#S4-295), Classic Squares LG (#S4-126)
- Die-cutting and embossing machine
- Pink glitter glue
- Tape: adhesive foam, cellophane, removable, double-sided

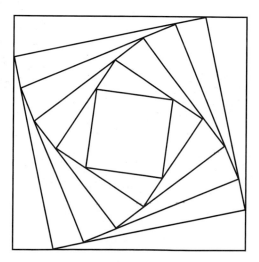

Iris-Folding Pattern

Materials

- Cardstock: olive green, coral, magenta, cream
- Ooh La La For Her 6 x 6 paper pad
- All Occasion Tags stamp set
- Dye ink pads: black, green
- Ribbons: 14¾ inches ½-inch-wide olive green silk, 15 inches ½-inch-wide magenta grosgrain, 8 inches ¼-inch-wide cream loopy
- Green/white baker's twine
- Large cream button
- 4 white self-adhesive pearls
- 2 light green self-adhesive gems
- Grommet Tags die templates (#S4-322)
- Die-cutting machine
- Hot-glue gun
- Adhesive foam squares
- Quick-drying paper adhesive

My Friend

Design by **Keri Lee Sereika**

Form a 4½ x 4½-inch card from olive green cardstock.

Cut a 5¼ x 2-inch piece from dotted printed paper and a 5¼ x 2¾-inch piece from floral printed paper. Adhere to card front as shown.

Cut a 5⅕ x ⅞-inch piece from magenta cardstock. Wrap cream loopy ribbon around magenta piece; secure ends to back. Adhere to card front as shown.

Using green ink, stamp label onto cream cardstock. Stamp sentiment and butterfly onto label with black ink. Die-cut a 2⅞ x 1½-inch Grommet Tags tag around stamped label. Attach to card front using foam squares. Attach a pearl to both ends of label.

Adhere a 2 x 2-inch piece of cream cardstock to a 2¼ x 2¼-inch piece of coral cardstock. Adhere to upper left corner of card front with foam squares.

Cut five 3-inch lengths of magenta ribbon. Referring to photo, fold each length in half creating loops; hot glue ends together to secure. Referring to photos, overlap ends of loops and adhere to center of cream square on card front to create flower petals.

Thread button with baker's twine. Tie a knot on back and trim ends. Adhere to center of flower.

Cut a 2¾-inch length of olive green ribbon; cut a v-notch at one end. Adhere opposite end of ribbon below flower. Tie a double-loop bow with remaining olive green ribbon. Adhere below flower as shown.

Embellish card with remaining pearls and gems.

Sources: Paper pad from My Mind's Eye; stamp set from Gina K. Designs; dye ink pads from Imagine Crafts/Tsukineko; baker's twine from The Twinery; self-adhesive pearls and gems from Queen & Co.; die templates from Spellbinders™ Paper Arts; foam squares from SCRAPBOOK ADHESIVES BY 3L™; quick-drying paper adhesive from Beacon Adhesives Inc.

Fabulous Flowers

Ranging in size, color, shape and texture, flowers are everywhere. In prints, in fabrics, on clothing or on tables in vases, flowers are quintessential to design everywhere, paper crafting included. With an endless list of ways to alter or create floral accents, finding ways to embellish a project using beautiful blossoms can be both exciting and fulfilling.

Triple Floral Thank You

Design by **Jing-Jing Nickel**

Form a 4¼ x 5½-inch card from light blue cardstock.

Cut a 4 x 5⅛-inch piece from black cardstock. Cut a 3 x 4-inch piece from fabric paper and a 1⅜ x 4-inch piece from Dresses paper. Layer and adhere to black cardstock piece as shown.

Cut a 4 x 1½-inch piece from Fabric paper. Punch border along top edge. Adhere to black cardstock panel as shown. Attach to card front using foam squares.

Layer and attach stickers to card front as shown.

Die-cut a Large Rolled Rose from felt. Following manufacturer's instructions, roll rose and secure with adhesive. Adhere to card front as shown. Attach gem flower to center of felt rose. Adhere paper flowers around felt rose as desired. 🐛

Sources: *Cardstock from Bazzill Basics Paper Inc.; printed papers and Phrase Stickers from Crate Paper Inc.; remaining sticker set from SRM Press Inc.; felt from EK Success; medium paper flowers from Prima Marketing Inc.; small paper flowers from Maya Road; border punch from Fiskars; die from My Favorite Things; foam squares from GlueArts; paper adhesive from Helmar.*

Materials

- Cardstock: light blue, black
- Emma's Shoppe printed papers: Fabric, Dresses
- Aqua wool felt
- Sticker sets: Emma's Shoppe Phrase Stickers, Fancy Sticker Sentiment Thanks
- Light blue self-adhesive gem flower
- Paper flowers: 1 medium turquoise, 1 medium aqua, 3 small white
- Scallop Sentiment Border Punch
- Large Rolled Rose die
- Die-cutting machine
- Adhesive foam squares
- Paper adhesive

Materials

- Cardstock: red, yellow
- Printed papers:
  Schoolhouse Workbook,
  Schoolhouse No. 2 Pencil,
  Schoolhouse Flashcards
  Report Card Wild Cards
- Label sticker
- Tag-its #6 stamp set
- Dye ink pads: red, green,
  black, dark brown
- Twine
- Old blue jeans
- Star dies or punches
- Bone folder
- Foam pad
- Quick-drying fabric glue
- Paper adhesive

2good2be Forgotten

Design by **Sherry Wright**

Form a 4½ x 5¾-inch card from red cardstock.

Cut a 4¼ x 5½-inch piece from Flashcards paper. Cut a 1⅝ x 5¼-inch piece from Workbook paper and a 1 x 4¾-inch piece from No. 2 Pencil paper. Adhere printed paper pieces to Flashcards panel. Cut "Learn" card from Wild Card paper. Adhere to Flashcards panel as shown.

Wrap twine around Flashcards panel as shown. Tie bow and trim ends. Adhere panel to card front.

Stamp sentiment onto label sticker with black ink. Using green and red ink, stamp apple next to sentiment. Attach sticker to card front as shown.

Tear an approximately 15 x 1¼-inch piece from old blue jeans. Create a Rolled Ribbon Rose from denim strip using quick-drying fabric glue. Trim blue jean strip as needed when desired size rose has been created. Attach to card front as shown.

Create two 3-D Cardstock Stars from a 1⅝-inch-wide red cardstock star and a 1-inch-wide yellow cardstock star. Ink scored lines black and dark brown as desired. Attach to card front as shown. ✏

Sources: *Cardstock from Bazzill Basics Paper Inc.; printed papers from October Afternoon; label sticker from Jenni Bowlin Studio; stamp set from Papertrey Ink; quick-drying fabric glue from Beacon Adhesives Inc.*

Materials

- Kraft cardstock
- Life's Journey paper pad
- Cream tissue paper
- Distress ink pads: brown, light brown
- Ribbon: 21 inches ½-inch-wide white seam binding, 7 inches ³⁄₁₆-inch-wide brown/cream gingham
- Gold/black decorative brad
- ⅝-inch circle punch
- Blossoms Three die templates (#S4-312)
- Die-cutting machine
- Paper piercer
- Sewing machine
- White thread
- Double-sided tape

Tissue-Paper Flower Card

Design by **Nina Brackett**

Form a 4⅛ x 5½-inch card from cardstock.

Cut a 4 x 5¼-inch piece from pink printed paper. Adhere a 2 x 5¼-inch piece of cream printed paper to pink panel as shown. Using circle punch, punch a half-circle centered at top and bottom of layered panel.

Cut a 7-inch length from seam binding. Wrap vertically around panel as shown; secure ends to back. Adhere to card front.

Zigzag-stitch along side edges of panel.

Fold a large piece of tissue paper in half; continue folding until you have 10–12 layers of paper. Using 2⅝-inch Blossoms Three die template, cut a flower from layered tissue paper. Repeat using 1⅞-inch and 1⅛-inch Blossoms Three die templates.

Stack flowers on top of each other. Pierce a hole through center of flowers and insert brad. Trim between petals as desired. Pinch flower layers toward center to add dimension.

Hand-cut two leaves from text printed paper. Add color with brown and light brown ink. Pinch leaves at center to create dimension. Layer and adhere leaves and flower to card front as shown.

Ink remaining seam binding lightly with dark brown ink. Tie a double bow and trim ends. Tie a bow with gingham ribbon; trim ends. Layer and adhere bows to card front below flower. ❧

Sources: *Cardstock from Gina K. Designs; paper pad from K&Company; distress ink pads from Ranger Industries Inc.; brad and circle punch from Stampin' Up!; die templates from Spellbinders™ Paper Arts; double-sided tape from Scor-Pal Products.*

Thinking of You

Design by **Sherry Wright**

Project note: *Ink edges of cut pieces dark brown unless instructed otherwise.*

Form a 4⅜ x 5⅝-inch card from aqua cardstock; do not ink edges.

Cut a 4¼ x 5½-inch piece from Precious Motif paper. Cut a 1¾ x 5⅛-inch piece from Precious Motif paper and a 2¼ x 4⅝-inch piece from Everywhere Correspond paper. Layer and adhere pieces to card front as shown. Cut off edge of doily and adhere to left edge of card front.

Stamp frame onto Boyish Plaid paper with dark brown ink. Stamp "thinking of you" inside frame with blue ink. Cut out frame; adhere to card front as shown.

Apply a small circle of fabric glue to white cardstock. Using turquoise lace, begin rolling and pressing lace into adhesive. Continue until lace flower is desired size; trim ends of lace. Let dry completely. Cut out lace flower. Repeat twice using light aqua lace.

Layer and adhere lace flowers and flower bouquet to card front as shown. Embellish lace flowers with pearls as desired.

Ink bird embellishment dark brown. Adhere to bottom edge of sentiment frame. ❧

Sources: *Cardstock from Papertrey Ink; printed papers and stamp set from My Mind's Eye; flower bouquet from Melissa Frances; self-adhesive pearls from Zva Creative; quick-drying fabric glue and paper adhesive from Beacon Adhesives Inc.*

Materials

- Cardstock: aqua, white
- Spring Florals stamp set
- Lost and Found 2 Breeze printed papers: Precious Motif, Everywhere Correspond, Boyish Plaid
- White paper dolly
- Stamps: "thinking of you," Lost & Found 2 Sunshine set
- Dye ink pads: dark brown, blue
- Lace: light aqua, turquoise
- Small white flower bouquet
- White self-adhesive pearls
- White bird embellishment
- Quick-drying fabric glue
- Quick-drying paper adhesive

Elegant Headband

Design by **Heidi Blankenship**

Using various Rose Creations flower die templates, cut multiple flowers from felt.

Layer and adhere flowers together using hot-glue gun, applying glue to centers of flowers only.

In the same manner, attach decorative embellishment and pearl to center of layered felt flower. Attach flower to headband using hot-glue gun. ✿☙

Sources: *Felt from Jo-Ann Stores Inc.; self-adhesive pearl from Want2Scrap; decorative embellishment from Bo-Bunny Press; die templates from Spellbinders™ Paper Arts.*

Materials

- Ribbon-covered headband
- Ivory 50% wool felt
- Large cream self-adhesive pearl
- Bronze decorative embellishment
- Rose Creations die templates (#S5-050)
- Die-cutting machine
- Hot-glue gun

Paper Pretties

The use of paper to embellish is often overlooked, underutilized and underappreciated. From the elementary use of a tag or simple layering beneath a stamped image, to a more intricate application of cutting and scoring to create a paper medallion or hand-cut leaf, using paper elements can be a very cost-effective and effortless way to create striking embellishments time and time again.

Cherish Trio

Designs by **Sharon M. Reinhart**

Paper Die-Cut Flowers

Project note: *This flower-making technique will be used in Frame, Mini Tote Bag and Photo/Note Cube.*

Die-cut three 1⅜-inch scalloped circles, one from Floral Ledger paper and two from iridescent cream printed paper. Spray each scalloped circle lightly with water. Crumple and crinkle circles with fingers. Flatten circles out and stack on top of each other. Pierce a hole through center of circles and insert a brad. Crumple up layers toward center, covering brad. Spray lightly with water again; let dry. Gently separate layers until desired look has been achieved, creating a paper flower. Ink edges rust.

Apply a small amount of dimensional gloss medium to center of flower. Press seed beads into gloss medium and let dry.

Frame

Ink edges of frame olive green; let dry.

Adhere a 4½ x 4½-inch piece of Floral Ledger paper to front of frame as shown. Flip frame over; remove back of frame and clear insert. Using craft knife, cut out window opening from printed paper. Replace clear insert and frame back. Lightly sand all edges of frame. Ink edges rust.

Die-cut and emboss a 1⅜ x 2⅛-inch label from Floral Ledger paper; ink edges rust. Wrap a small piece of lace around label, securing ends to back.

Cut a 2½-inch length of ribbon; trim ends at an angle. Fold in half and adhere to back of label.

Cut a 2¼ x 2¼-inch piece from parchment paper; ink rust. Punch a heart from inked paper. Adhere to lace-covered label.

Set label onto foam pad; use paper piercer to pierce holes along outside edge of heart. Insert thread through beading needle. Beginning from back side, slide needle through a hole on parchment heart and label. Secure end of thread to back of label with tape. Slide bead onto threaded needle and pass needle back down through same hole. Thread needle through next hole from back to front; slide bead onto

Materials

- Wooden pieces: mini tote box, 4½-inch frame, 2-inch photo/note cube
- Printed papers: Je t'Adore Floral Ledger, iridescent cream
- Chipboard
- Parchment paper
- Chalk ink pads: olive green, rust
- Cream acrylic paint
- 15½ inches ¼-inch-wide green sheer ribbon
- 1½-inch-wide white lace trim
- 7 copper mini brads
- Peach seed beads
- Beading needle with light brown metallic thread
- Lace Scallop Heart Large punch
- Die templates: Elegant Flourishes (#656639), Labels Four (#S4-190), Classic Scalloped Circles SM (#S4-125)
- Die-cutting and embossing machine
- Paper piercer
- Spray bottle with water
- Craft knife
- Foam paintbrush
- Craft sponge
- Sanding block
- Foam pad
- Adhesive foam tape
- Double-sided tape
- Tape
- Clear dimensional gloss medium
- Glue stick

needle and pass back through same hole. Continue in the same manner until all holes have been beaded. Trim excess thread and secure to back of label with tape. Attach label to frame as shown with foam tape.

Using smaller Elegant Flourish die, die-cut a flourish from chipboard; ink olive green using craft sponge. Adhere to right side of frame.

Following Paper Die-Cut Flower instructions, create a flower. Adhere to frame as shown.

Place desired sentiment or photo inside frame.

Mini Tote Bag

Lightly sand wooden tote bag. Using foam paintbrush, paint tote cream; let dry. Add second coat of paint if needed. Ink handle edges rust.

Following Paper Die-Cut Flowers instructions, create three flowers. Set flowers aside.

Cut two 4¼ x 3⅝-inch pieces from Floral Ledger paper; ink edges rust. Adhere to front and back of tote. Ink edges of tote rust.

Using smaller Elegant Flourish die, die-cut a flourish from chipboard; ink olive green using craft sponge. Adhere to tote as shown.

In the same manner as for Frame, create a layered tag from Floral Ledger paper using 1¾ x 3⅛-inch Labels

Four die template. Attach label to frame as shown, using foam tape.

Adhere flowers to tote front as desired.

Photo/Note Cube

Lightly sand wooden cube and wipe off.

Using foam paintbrush, paint cube cream; let dry. Apply second coat if needed.

Cut four 2 x 2-inch pieces from Floral Ledger paper. Adhere to sides of cube.

Cut four 1 x 2-inch pieces from Floral Ledger paper. Adhere pieces one at a time to top of cube around metal piece working in a clockwise manner and overlapping pieces. Using craft sponge, ink edges of cube rust.

Using smaller Elegant Flourish die, die-cut a flourish from chipboard; ink olive green using craft sponge. Cut in half and adhere a half to front and back of cube. **Note:** *If needed, trim chipboard flourish to fit cube.*

Following Paper Die-Cut Flowers instructions, create three flowers. Adhere to top of cube as shown.

In the same manner as for Frame, create a label from Floral Ledger paper. Attach label to cube as shown, using foam tape.

Cut three 3½-inch lengths of ribbon. Wrap ribbons around metal photo/note holder and knot. Trim ends at an angle. ❧

Sources: *Wooden pieces from Michaels Stores Inc.; Je t'Adore Floral Ledger printed paper from Making Memories; chalk ink pad from Clearsnap Inc.; punch from Martha Stewart Crafts; Elegant Flourishes die templates from Sizzix; remaining die templates from Spellbinders™ Paper Arts; paper piercer and Glossy Accents clear dimensional gloss medium from Ranger Industries Inc.; double-sided tape from Scor-Pal Products.*

Materials

- Cardstock: dark brown, white, orange
- Aqua felt
- Six by Six Honey Cake paper pad
- Sunny Days stamp set
- Dark brown dye ink pad
- 23 inches ½-inch-wide brown satin ribbon
- 7 inches 1-inch-wide white lace trim
- Brown/white baker's twine
- Silver decorative button
- Sewing machine
- Brown thread
- Dies: Charming Oval set (#VSDC-008), Jotted Heart (#VSDC-005)
- Die-cutting machine
- Adhesive foam squares
- Clear dimensional gloss medium
- Double-sided tape

Treasure

Design by **Teresa Kline**

Form a 4¼ x 5½-inch card from dark brown cardstock.

Cut a 4⅛ x 4¾-inch piece from brown floral paper. Cut two 3 x 2-inch pieces from blue/white striped paper and one 5½ x 2-inch piece from orange/white dot paper. Create pleated strips from striped and dot printed paper pieces. Machine-stitch pleated pieces together as shown. Referring to photo, adhere sewn pieces to brown floral panel 1 inch above bottom edge.

Wrap lace trim around panel as shown; wrap and secure ends to back. Wrap ribbon around panel as shown; tie a double bow and trim ends. Adhere panel to card front, allowing pleated paper pieces to hang free.

Attach button to center of bow using dimensional gloss medium.

Using Jotted Heart die, cut a heart from aqua felt. Wrap two lengths of baker's twine around heart as shown. Holding lengths together, tie a bow and trim ends. Attach heart to card front using foam squares.

Stamp sentiment onto white cardstock. Using 1⅞ x ¾-inch Charming Oval die, cut a decorative oval around sentiment. Die-cut a 2 x ⅞-inch decorative oval from orange cardstock. Layer and attach ovals to card front using foam squares. 🐾

Sources: Cardstock and Crystal Effects clear dimensional gloss medium from Stampin' Up!; paper pad from My Mind's Eye; stamp set and dies from Verve Stamps; baker's twine from The Twinery; idea-ology Tim Holtz button from Ranger Industries Inc.; adhesive foam squares from SCRAPBOOK ADHESIVES BY 3L™; double-sided tape from Scor-Pal Products.

Melody of Love

Design by **Jessica Fick**

Die-cut two 4⅛-inch scalloped circles from heavy white cardstock. Score a vertical line ¾ inch below top edge of one scalloped circle. Aligning edges, adhere ¾-inch flap to remaining scalloped circle to form a 4⅛-inch scalloped-circle card.

Using 3½-inch Standard Circles SM die template, cut a circle from printed paper. Using 3¾-inch Standard Circles LG die template, cut a circle from black cardstock. Adhere circles together. Zigzag-stitch around edge of printed paper circle. Adhere to card front.

Stamp sentiment onto white smooth cardstock with black ink. Using desired Grommet Tags die template, die-cut and emboss a tag around sentiment; leave die template in place. Ink tag gray using blending tool; remove die template. Adhere to card front as shown.

Stamp bird on branch onto white smooth cardstock. Color using markers and cut out. Attach to card front using foam dots.

Tie a bow with ribbon; trim ends using pinking shears. Attach bow to card front using adhesive dots.

Die-cut a large rolled rose from felt. Following manufacturer's instructions, roll felt into rose shape and secure with paper adhesive. Punch three leaves from green cardstock. Layer and adhere leaves and felt rose to bow using adhesive dots as needed.

Color pearl using desired marker; let dry. Attach to left edge of sentiment tag. ✎

Sources: *Heavyweight cardstock from Gina K. Designs; white smooth cardstock and markers from Imagination International Inc.; green cardstock and leaf punch from Stampin' Up!; stamp set from Sweet 'n Sassy Stamps; distress ink pad and blending tool from Ranger Industries Inc.; Large Rolled Roses die from My Favorite Things; remaining die templates from Spellbinders™ Paper Arts; scoring board and tool and double-sided tape from Scor-Pal Products; adhesive dots from Glue Dots.*

Materials

- Cardstock: white heavyweight, white smooth, green
- Victoria Gardens Botanical Ballad printed paper
- Blue felt
- Peace of God stamp set
- Dye ink pads: black, gray distress
- Copic® markers: B91, B93, B95, E33, E35, E40, E41, E43, R32, R39, YG91, YG93, YG95
- 11 inches 1¼-inch-wide black silk ribbon
- White self-adhesive pearl
- Leaf punch
- Die templates: Classic Scalloped Circles LG (#S4-124), Standard Circles SM (#S4-116), Standard Circles LG (#S4-114), Grommet Tags (#S4-322), Large Rolled Roses
- Die-cutting and embossing machine
- Blending tool
- Scoring board with tool
- Pinking shears
- Sewing machine
- White thread
- Adhesive foam dots
- Adhesive dots
- Double-sided tape
- Paper adhesive

aper
Pretties

Materials

- Pink cardstock
- 5th Avenue printed papers: Octavia, Essie
- 5th Avenue Ephemera Stickers
- 1⅜-inch chipboard scalloped circle tag
- "A happy heart" sentiment rub-on transfer
- Light brown dye ink pad
- Copic® markers: RV11, YG91
- White acrylic paint
- Iridescent glitter
- 25 inches ½-inch-wide light green seam binding
- 3⅜ inches ⅝-inch-wide white lace
- White string
- Light brown ribbon flower
- Silver self-adhesive gem
- 9–12 cream buttons, various sizes
- White resin frame
- Craft knife
- Paintbrush
- Sewing machine
- Light green thread
- Spray adhesive
- Quick-drying fabric adhesive

A Happy Heart

Design by **Melissa Phillips**

Form a 3¾ x 5¼-inch card from cardstock. Paint edges white; let dry.

Cut a 3⅜ x 3-inch piece from Octavia paper and a 3⅜ x 2-inch piece from Essie paper; ink edges light brown. Layer and adhere to card front as shown. Adhere lace over printed paper seam and machine-stitch along edge of printed papers.

Use craft knife to cut a ½-inch slit through fold of card 2 inches from bottom of card. Insert seam binding through slit and around card; tie a multiple-loop bow and trim ends. Lightly ink bow light brown.

Thread 9–10 buttons with white string; tie knots on back sides and trim ends. Adhere buttons along bottom edge of seam binding as shown.

Attach desired sticker inside resin frame. Adhere frame to card front as shown. Adhere ribbon flower to upper right corner of frame; attach gem to flower center.

Apply sentiment rub-on transfer onto chipboard tag. Color sentiment as desired with markers. Spray adhesive onto tag and sprinkle with glitter. Ink edges light brown. Thread one button with white string; thread string through hole on tag and around seam binding bow. Tie knot on back and trim ends. ✿

Sources: *Printed papers, stickers and resin frame from Melissa Frances; markers from Imagination International Inc.; spray adhesive from Krylon; quick-drying fabric adhesive from Beacon Adhesives Inc.*

Recycled Elegance

Design by **Linda Lucas**

Project note: *Ink edges of all cut pieces dark brown.*

Form a 4 x 6-inch card from dark brown cardstock.

Cut a 3¼ x 5½-inch piece from white cardstock; tear off bottom edge. Emboss white panel using Framed Tulips embossing folder.

Using Regal Flourishes embossing folder, emboss a 3¼ x 4-inch piece of blue printed paper. Adhere to embossed white panel as shown.

Using 2¾ x 4⅜-inch Labels Four die template, cut a label from brown printed paper. Using Square Lattice embossing folder, emboss label. Adhere to layered panel.

Use computer with printer to generate vintage perfume ad image onto white cardstock. Using 2⅝ x 3⅜-inch Labels Eighteen die template, cut and emboss a label around image. Attach to layered panel using foam tape.

Cut a 6 x 1¼-inch piece from text paper. Create a pleated strip from text paper piece. Adhere to layered panel as shown.

Cut a 6-inch length from seam binding. Wrap around layered panel above pleated paper strip. Adhere panel to card front.

Using an 8-inch length of seam binding, tie a bow. Trim ends and adhere to card front as shown.

Punch three 1⅜-inch circles from text paper. Layer and adhere to card front over bow.

To create circle embellishment, punch a 1-inch circle from text paper. Apply paper adhesive to center of circle. Twist and wrap a length of seam binding onto top of adhesive-covered circle, pressing seam binding into adhesive as needed. When desired look is achieved, trim seam binding. Layer and adhere button and brad on top of circle. Adhere to card front as shown.

Embellish card with pearls as desired. ❧

Sources: *Digital stamp from The Graphics Fairy; distress ink pad and Damask & Regal Flourishes embossing folder set from Ranger Industries Inc.; remaining embossing folders from Stampin' Up!; die templates from Spellbinders™ Paper Arts; double-sided tape from Imagination International Inc.; paper adhesive from Tombow USA.*

Materials

- Cardstock: dark brown, white
- Printed papers: blue, brown, text
- Vintage perfume ad digital stamp*
- Dark brown distress ink pad
- 28 inches ½-inch-wide light aqua seam binding
- Gold decorative button
- Pearl brad
- 5 white self-adhesive pearls
- Circle punches: 1⅜-inch, 1-inch
- Embossing folders: Square Lattice (#119976), Framed Tulips (#121809), Damask & Regal Flourishes set (#SAL656648)
- Die templates: Labels Four (#S4-190), Labels Eighteen (#S4-310)
- Die-cutting and embossing machine
- Adhesive foam tape
- Double-sided tape
- Paper adhesive
- Computer with printer

*Digital stamp available at: http://graphicsfairy.blogspot.com/2011/01/antique-ephemera-amazing-romantic.html

Materials

- Cardstock: olive green, red, gold metallic
- Chiyogami printed paper
- Gold Starform Glitter Dot Peel-Off stickers
- "Merry Christmas" stamp
- Red chalk ink pad
- Red fine-tip marker
- 8 inches ½-inch-wide brown seam binding
- Apron Lace border punch
- Die templates: Petite Ovals SM (#S4-140), Nested Lacey Pennants (#S5-029)
- Die-cutting and embossing machine
- Wooden skewer
- Adhesive foam tape
- Double-sided tape
- Glue stick

Oh! Christmas Tree

Design by **Sharon M. Reinhart**

Form a 4½ x 5½-inch card from olive green cardstock.

Cut a 4½ x 5½-inch piece from red cardstock. Using border punch, punch both long edges of red panel. Adhere to card front. Adhere a 3¾ x 5½-inch piece of printed paper to card front.

To create tree, use desired Nested Lacey Pendants die template to die-cut a pendant from olive green cardstock. Adhere glitter dot stickers to tree as shown.

Wrap seam binding around center of tree threading seam binding through lacey cutouts. Tie bow on front and trim ends. Attach to card front using foam tape.

Stamp "Merry Christmas" onto gold metallic cardstock. Die-cut and emboss a 2 x ⅞-inch oval around sentiment. Draw a border around die cut using fine-tip marker. Adhere to card front as shown. Embellish sentiment oval with glitter dot stickers.

To create paper bead, cut a 1 x 7-inch strip from printed paper. Cut strip in half diagonally creating two long triangles. Lightly dampen wide end of one triangle; place wide end of triangle on skewer and wrap paper around skewer. Apply glue onto last 1 inch of triangle and finish wrapping. Slide paper off of wooden skewer and adhere below tree on card front, creating a Christmas tree base. ❧

Sources: *Cardstock from Bazzill Basics Paper Inc. and Michaels Stores Inc.; Chiyogami printed paper from The Japanese Paper Place; stickers from Elizabeth Craft Designs; border punch from Fiskars; die templates from Spellbinders™ Paper Arts; die-cutting and embossing machine from Sizzix; foam tape from 3M.*

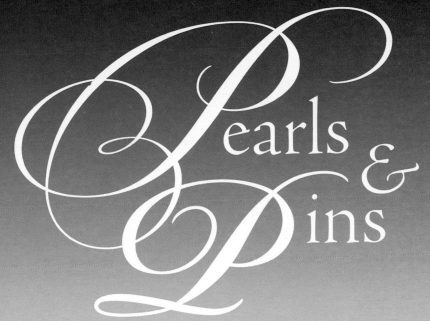

Pearls & Pins

A bit of bling, shimmer and shine, that is what pearls and pins are all about! Creating decorative embellishments from beads and straight pins is an inventive way to add interest and personal style without breaking the bank. Preening with pearls is an exceptional way to add shimmer and shine without overwhelming existing elements. Whether using a swirl of pearls as a focal piece or just one pin as an accent, no one can resist the beauty and glamour these feminine embellishments express.

Butterfly Love

Design by **Nina Brackett**

Form a 4¼ x 5½-inch card from dark blue cardstock.

Cut a 3¼ x 5⅜-inch piece from Dew Drops paper. Referring to photo, curl upper and lower right corners of paper. Cut a 1 x 5⅜-inch piece from Flower Blooms paper. Using dark blue ink, stamp background text onto Flower Blooms piece. Adhere printed paper pieces to card front as shown.

Wrap ribbon around card front covering paper seam. Tie bow; trim ends. Attach brad to bow.

Using black ink, stamp butterfly onto white smooth cardstock. Color using markers; cut out.

String pearls onto embroidery floss. Wrap beaded strand around center of butterfly; knot on back and trim ends. Attach butterfly to card front using foam tape.

Using dark blue ink, stamp "i love you" onto card front. Attach a pearl to both sides of sentiment. ❧

Sources: *Cardstock from Papertrey Ink; printed papers and die cuts from Pink Paislee; stamps from Layers of Color; markers from Imagination International Inc.; pearl beads from Darice Inc.; double-sided tape from Scor-Pal Products.*

Materials

- Cardstock: dark blue, white smooth
- Butterfly Garden printed papers: Dew Drops, Flower Blooms
- Butterfly Garden Ephemera die cuts: flower
- Stamps: Embroidered Butterfly, The Love Chapter set
- Dye ink pads: black, dark blue
- Copic® markers: B91, B95, B97, Y35
- 20 inches ⅜-inch-wide blue/white dot ribbon
- White embroidery floss
- Gold decorative brad
- 6 (4mm) white pearl beads
- 2 small white self-adhesive pearls
- Adhesive foam tape
- Double-sided tape

Your Friendship

Design by **Jing-Jing Nickel**

Form a 4¼ x 5-inch card from cardstock.

Cut two 4¼ x 1-inch paper pieces, one from Mid-Summer Nights Dots paper and one from Flower Burst paper. Adhere to card front as shown.

Adhere rickrack over printed paper seam as shown.

Adhere Flower Burst paper to chipboard butterfly; trim excess paper as needed and sand edges. Insert stickpins into top of butterfly as shown. Attach butterfly to card front.

Stamp sentiment above butterfly. ✎

Sources: *Cardstock from Bazzill Basics Paper Inc.; printed papers from Little Yellow Bicycle; chipboard butterfly and rickrack from Maya Road; stamp set from Unity Stamp Co.; stickpins from Jenni Bowlin Studio.*

Materials

- Blue-gray cardstock
- Fresh Print Traveler printed papers: Navy Wide Stripe/Mid-Summer Nights Dots, Round a'bout/Small Flower Burst
- Chipboard butterfly
- The Best is Yet To Be stamp set (KOM 2/11)
- Black dye ink pad
- 4½ inches ¼-inch-wide green felt rickrack
- 2 red bead-tipped stickpins
- Sandpaper
- Adhesive foam dots
- Paper adhesive

Paris

Design by **Heidi Blankenship**

Form a 5½ x 5½-inch card from dark brown cardstock.

Cut a 5¼ x 5¼-inch piece from cream cardstock; ink edges light brown. Using dark brown ink, stamp images and sentiment onto cream panel as shown. Adhere to card front.

Using 2⅜ x 1⅞-inch and 3⅜ x 4⅜-inch Classic Rectangles LG die templates, cut and emboss a frame from pearl craft foil. **Note:** *Use removable tape to secure die templates in place.* Using embossing folder, emboss foil frame. Sand frame using sanding block. Adhere to card front as shown using hot-glue gun.

Attach pearls and flourishes to card as shown, saving one pearl for button. Layer and adhere crochet flowers, button and pearl to card front. ❧

Sources: *Stamp sets from JustRite; craft foil, die templates and die-cutting machine from Spellbinders™ Paper Arts; distress ink pad from Ranger Industries Inc.; self-adhesive pearls from Want2Scrap; buttons from Bo-Bunny Press; removable tape from 3M; double-sided adhesive from SCRAPBOOK ADHESIVES BY 3L™.*

Materials

- Cardstock: dark brown, cream
- Precious Metals Premium Craft Foils Assortment: Pearl
- Stamp sets: Bon Voyage, Greetings from Paris
- Dye ink pads: dark brown, light brown distress
- Self-adhesive pearls: white flourishes, 5 medium light pink, 3 small light pink
- Et Cetera Buttons: glitter
- Crochet flowers: 1 large cream, 1 medium light brown
- Die templates: Classic Rectangles LG (#S4-132), Grand Rectangles (#LF-132)
- Grand Calibur™
- Sanding block
- Removable tape
- Hot-glue gun
- Double-sided adhesive

Materials

- Cream cardstock
- Printed papers: Stella & Rose Hattie Buddies Argyle, Stella & Rose Gertie Little One Darling Dots, Stella & Rose Gertie You & Me Numbers, First Edition Specialty Designer Series text, blue
- Rainbow & Cloud stamp and die set
- Black dye ink pad
- Clear embossing powder
- 4¼ inches 1½-inch-wide Turquoise Bloomer ribbon
- Stickpins: 3 floral pearl, 2 butterfly
- Brackets die (#SAL656625)
- Die-cutting machine
- Embossing heat tool
- Chain-nose pliers
- Sandpaper
- Sewing machine
- Brown thread
- Dimensional gloss medium
- Adhesive foam squares
- Double-sided tape

Made my Day

Design by **Teresa Kline**

Form a 4¼ x 5½-inch card from white cardstock.

Cut a 4⅛ x 1½-inch piece from blue printed paper. Using Bracket die, cut bottom edge. Cut a 4⅛ x 3-inch piece from Buddies Argyle paper and a 4⅛ x 1½-inch piece from text paper. Referring to photo, layer and adhere printed paper pieces together.

Using sewing machine, zigzag-stitch along top edge of layered panel.

Stamp sentiment onto You & Me Numbers paper. Sprinkle with embossing powder; heat-emboss. Cut a rectangle around sentiment and cut a V-notch at right end. Sand edges. Using sewing machine and referring to photo, zigzag-stitch sentiment to layered panel. Adhere to card front.

Using small and large cloud dies, cut clouds from Darling Dots paper. Attach to card front using foam squares.

Attach ribbon to card front as shown using double-sided tape.

Using chain-nose pliers, bend each floral stickpin ¼ inch from decorative end. Insert bent stickpins into ribbon as shown. Slide butterfly stickpins into top of ribbon. Secure stickpins with dimensional gloss medium as needed. 🌿

Sources: *Cardstock from Papertrey Ink; Stella & Rose printed papers from My Mind's Eye; text printed paper and Crystal Effects dimensional gloss medium from Stampin' Up!; stamp and die set from Lil' Inker Designs; Bloomer Ribbon and stickpins from Webster's Pages; Tim Holtz Bracket die from Ranger Industries Inc.; foam squares from SCRAPBOOK ADHESIVES BY 3L™; double-sided tape from Scor-Pal Products.*

Heartfelt Birthday Wishes

Design by Jing-Jing Nickel

Form a 5½ x 4¼-inch card from cardstock.

Cut a 5¼ x 1⅜-inch piece from Raspberry Syrup paper and a 5¼ x 2⅝-inch piece from Lemon Zest paper. Layer and adhere to card front as shown.

Die-cut a bracket border from a 5½ x ⅜-inch piece of Zesty paper. Adhere to card front as shown.

Attach sentiment sticker and round Cherry label sticker to card front as shown.

Die-cut a large rolled rose from felt. Roll flower following manufacturer's instructions. Layer and adhere velvet leaves and flower to card front as shown, using foam dot to attach flower. Insert stickpins into flower as shown. ✎

Sources: *Cardstock from Bazzill Basics Paper Inc.; printed papers from BasicGrey; wool felt from EK Success; sentiment stickers from SRM Press Inc.; round Cherry label sticker from October Afternoon; velvet leaves and jewel-tipped stickpin from Maya Road; butterfly stickpin from Jenni Bowlin Studio; dies from My Favorite Things; die-cutting machine from Provo Craft.*

Materials

- Lime green cardstock
- Hello Luscious printed papers: Lemon Zest, Raspberry Syrup, Zesty
- Purple wool felt
- Fancy Sticker Sentiment Birthday
- Cherry Hill Word Stickers: round cherry label sticker
- 2 green velvet leaves
- Stickpins: 3 jewel-tipped, butterfly
- Dies: Large Rolled Rose, Open Bracket Border
- Die-cutting machine
- Adhesive dots
- Paper adhesive

Notable *Naturals*

There is no beauty so perfectly expressed as the pure and sincere beauty we find in nature itself. Using materials derived from natural products as well as nature's own embellishments is a wonderful way to have a project really stand out. As simple as using a shell-toned button topped with a pearl, or as intricate as adding a feather as a finishing touch, nature is sure to inspire, delight and simply embellish.

Materials

- Cardstock: kraft, ivory
- Printed papers: Stella & Rose Mabel Little Lady Posies, Stella & Rose Mabel So Sweet Plait Die-Cut, Lost and Found 2 Rosy Remember Dots
- Autumn Splendor stamp set
- Black distress ink pad
- 4 inches ¼-inch-wide burnt orange rickrack
- 6 inches 1¾-inch-wide burlap strip
- Burlap string
- 18 inches ⅝-inch-wide black twill ribbon
- Cream button
- Mini Tabs Foursome die set
- Die-cutting machine
- Sewing machine
- Black thread
- Adhesive foam squares
- Clear dimensional gloss medium
- Double-sided tape

Autumn Greetings

Design by **Teresa Kline**

Form a 4½ x 5½-inch card from kraft cardstock.

Adhere a 4 x 2-inch piece of Dots paper to top of a 4 x 5½-inch piece of Posies paper.

Stamp sentiment onto ivory cardstock. Using desired Mini Tabs die, die-cut a tab around sentiment. Adhere to layered panel as shown.

Wrap burlap strip around layered panel as shown; secure ends to back. Adhere rickrack to panel, overlapping bottom edge of burlap. Zigzag-stitch along top edge of burlap.

Wrap a 6-inch length of twill ribbon around panel on top of burlap. Secure ends to back.

Referring to photo, machine-stitch two hills along bottom of panel. Stamp a small leaf and a large leaf onto layered panel to create trees. Adhere panel to card front.

In the same manner, stamp leaves onto Plait Die-Cut paper. Apply gloss medium onto second set of trees; let dry and cut out, trimming off stems. Attach over corresponding leaves on card front using foam squares.

Tie a double-loop bow with remaining ribbon; trim ends. Thread burlap string through button and wrap around bow; tie string into a large bow. Trim ends. Adhere layered bow to card front as shown. ✑

Sources: Cardstock from Papertrey Ink and Stampin' Up!; printed papers from My Mind's Eye; stamp set from Verve Stamps; distress ink pad from Ranger Industries Inc.; die set from My Favorite Things; adhesive foam squares from SCRAPBOOK ADHESIVES BY 3L™; Crystal Effects dimensional gloss medium from Stampin' Up!; double-sided tape from 3M.

Double Medallion Gift Box

Design by **Keri Lee Sereika**

Cut a piece of pink cardstock a little less than half the width of the gift box and long enough to wrap around the box. Using red ink, stamp roses onto pink piece. Wrap and adhere stamped piece around box.

Using black ink, stamp banner and sentiment onto cream cardstock. Cut out and ink edges black. Attach to box using foam squares.

Cut a 12 x 2-inch strip from cream floral paper. Place paper strip onto scoring board with long edge horizontal. Using scoring tool, Score vertical lines ½ inch apart along entire length of strip. Accordion-fold strip along scored lines. Overlap short ends of scored strip, forming a ring, and adhere in place; let dry completely. Press accordion-folded ring flat creating a medallion. Attach to box as shown using adhesive dots. Repeat process with a 12 x 1-inch piece of pink floral paper, attaching medallion on top of first medallion.

Layer and adhere buttons and pearl to top of medallions. ✂

Sources: Stamp sets from Layers of Color; ink pads from Imagine Crafts/Tsukineko; self-adhesive pearl from Want2Scrap; adhesive dots from Therm O Web Inc.; quick-drying paper adhesive from Beacon Adhesives Inc.

Materials

- Cardstock: cream, pink
- Printed papers: cream floral, pink floral
- Brown gift box
- Stamp sets: Sentimental Banners, Vintage Roses
- Ink pads: black fine-detail, red dye
- Cream self-adhesive pearl
- Buttons: 1 large red, 1 medium cream
- Scoring board with tool
- Adhesive foam squares
- Adhesive dots
- Quick-drying paper adhesive

Shells in Your Pocket

Design by **Keri Lee Sereika**

Materials

- Cardstock: kraft, cream, brown
- Stamp sets: A Year of Borders, Gifts From the Sea
- Pigment ink pads: black fine-detail, brown chalk
- Copic® marker: E55
- Ribbon: 12 inches 1¼-inch-wide tan paper raffia, 6 inches ⅝-inch-wide white lace
- Brown/white baker's twine
- Cream shell button
- White self-adhesive pearls: 1 large, 4 small
- Labels Eighteen die templates (#S4-310)
- Die-cutting and embossing machine
- Marker airbrush system
- Adhesive foam squares
- Adhesive dot
- Quick-drying paper adhesive

Form a 4½ x 6-inch card from kraft cardstock.

Cut a 4¼ x 5-inch piece from cream cardstock. Stamp seashell border multiple times onto cream panel with brown ink.

Adhere a 4¼ x 1-inch piece of brown cardstock to cream panel as shown. Wrap lace ribbon around layered panel on top of brown strip; wrap and secure ends to back. Adhere to card front.

Wrap raffia ribbon around top of card front; tie knot and trim ends.

Thread button with baker's twine; Using adhesive dot, attach button to knot on raffia ribbon.

Stamp sentiment onto cream cardstock with black ink. Using 2 x 2½-inch Labels Eighteen die template, cut a label around sentiment; leave die template in place. Color sentiment label using marker and airbrush system; remove die template. Attach to card front using foam squares.

Embellish card with pearls as shown. ✿

Sources: *Stamp sets from Gina K. Designs; pigment ink pads from Imagine Crafts/Tsukineko; marker and airbrush system from Imagination International Inc.; baker's twine from The Twinery; button from Want2Scrap; die templates from Spellbinders™ Paper Arts; adhesive foam squares from SCRAPBOOK ADHESIVES BY 3L™; adhesive dot from Therm O Web Inc.; quick-drying paper adhesive from Beacon Adhesives Inc.*

Thank You Very Much

Design by **Sherry Wright**

Form a 4½ x 5½-inch card from light aqua cardstock. Adhere a 4½ x 5½-inch piece of Groomed Traveler paper to card front.

Cut a 4 x 5⅛-inch piece from kraft cardstock. Paint edges white; let dry. Adhere to card front as shown.

Cut a 2⅝ x 4⅞-inch piece from Serenity paper; distress edges using sandpaper and ink edges dark brown. Adhere to card front.

Cut a 1⅜ x 5½-inch piece from cardboard; rip off top layer. Paint white as shown; let dry. Adhere to card front.

Cut out bird image from Restful Retreat paper. Paint edges white and let dry; adhere to card front as shown.

Using watermark ink, stamp circle onto aqua cardstock. Sprinkle with embossing powder and heat-emboss. Stamp sentiment inside embossed circle with dark brown ink. Cut out circle; distress edges. Adhere to card front as shown.

Referring to photo, apply a small circle of fabric glue onto card front where a bird's nest will be placed. Wrap twine into a circle over fabric glue, pressing twine into glue until desired-size nest is created; trim end of twine. Repeat two more times, creating desired sizes of nests. Embellish nests with pearls.

Sources: Cardstock from Bazzill Basics Paper Inc.; printed papers from Webster's Pages; stamp set from Papertrey Ink; self-adhesive pearls from Zva Creative; quick-drying fabric and paper adhesive from Beacon Adhesives Inc.

Materials

- Cardstock: light aqua, kraft, aqua
- Printed papers: Ladies & Gents Groomed Traveler, Country Estate Restful Retreat, Country Estate Serenity
- Cardboard
- White paper doily
- Tag-its #2 stamp set
- Ink pads: dark brown dye, watermark
- White embossing powder
- White paint
- Natural twine
- White self-adhesive pearls, various sizes
- Embossing heat tool
- Paintbrush
- Sandpaper
- Quick-drying fabric adhesive
- Quick-drying paper adhesive

Best Day Ever

Design by **Teresa Kline**

Form a 4¼ x 5½-inch card from kraft cardstock.

Cut a 4 x 5⅜-inch piece from printed paper; distress edges using distressing tool. Referring to photo, wrap fabric ribbon and lace around panel as shown; secure ends to back. Wrap twine around panel multiple times; secure ends to back. Adhere panel to card front.

Thread a long length of twine through button; tie a multiple-loop bow on back and trim ends. Adhere to card front as shown.

Stain chipboard circle star as desired; let dry. Lightly brush cream paint onto chipboard piece; let dry. Adhere to card front as shown. Apply gloss medium inside star; sprinkle with glitter. Press glitter into gloss medium as needed; let dry.

Cut a 5 x ⅞-inch piece from ivory cardstock; cut a V-notch at both ends. Center and stamp sentiment onto ivory strip. With long edge horizontal on work surface, score vertical lines 1 inch, 1¼ inches and 1½ inches from left and right ends. Valley-fold first two scored lines and mountain-fold third scored line, creating a popped-up sentiment banner. Referring to photo and using adhesive dots, attach ends of banner to card front. 🐛

Sources: Kraft cardstock from Papertrey Ink; ivory cardstock and distressing tool from Stampin' Up!; printed paper from My Mind's Eye; stamp set from Verve Stamps; waterbased stain from Ranger Industries Inc.; double-sided tape from Scor-Pal Products.

Materials

- Cardstock: kraft, ivory
- Union Square Home Sweet Home Love Glittered printed paper
- Chipboard circle star*
- Framed Wishes stamp set
- Red dye ink pad
- Blue distress waterbased stain
- Cream acrylic paint
- Clear chunky glitter
- 6 inches ½-inch-wide cream ribbon
- 6 inches 1¼-inch-wide brown/blue fabric ribbon
- Ivory twine
- Red button
- Distressing tool
- Paintbrush
- Scoring tool
- Clear dimensional gloss medium
- Adhesive dots
- Double-sided tape

*If chipboard circle star is not available, create your own by cutting a star shape out of chipboard and then trimming a circle around cut-out star.

Card Artists

Heidi Blankenship
http://embellished-dreams.blogspot.com/
Wonderful Friend, 31
Elegant Headband, 42
Paris, 54

Nina Brackett
http://ninabdesigns.blogspot.com/
Much Love, 28
Blessings, 30
Tissue-Paper Flower Card, 40
Butterfly Love, 52

Lori Craig
http://loricraig.blogs.splitcoaststampers.com/
Gnomie, 26

Jessica Fick
http://iembellish.blogspot.com/
Thankful for You, 25
Melody of Love, 47

Teresa Kline
http://paperieblooms.blogspot.com/
Glittered Butterfly, 21
Primitive Pumpkins, 33
Treasure, 46
Made my Day, 55
Autumn Greetings, 58
Best Day Ever, 62

Linda Lucas
http://lovelylindascraftcentral.blogspot.com/
Reminiscing, 22
Recycled Elegance, 49

Tami Mayberry
http://tamimayberry.blogspot.com/
Bright Birthday Wishes, 32

Jing-Jing Nickel
http://thislittleartofmine.blogspot.com/
Triple Floral Thank You, 38
Your Friendship, 53
Heartfelt Birthday Wishes, 56

Melissa Phillips
http://lilybeanpaperie.typepad.com/lilybeans_paperie/
Button Heart, 19
A Happy Heart, 48

Sharon M. Reinhart
http://www.smrdesigns.blogspot.com/
Welcome Baby, 35
Cherish Trio, 44
Oh! Christmas Tree, 50

Keri Lee Sereika
http://www.pinklemonade.typepad.com
Head in the Clouds, 24
Butterflies Gift Bag, 27
My Friend, 36
Double Medallion Gift Box, 59
Shells in Your Pocket, 60

Kandis Smith
http://www.mycreativetreasury.blogspot.com/
Vintage Card, 18

Sherry Wright
http://sherrywright.typepad.com/
Happy Birthday Buttons, 20
2good2be Forgotten, 39
Thinking of You, 41
Thank You Very Much, 61

Exquisite Embellishments for Paper Crafts

EDITOR Tanya Fox

CREATIVE DIRECTOR Brad Snow

PUBLISHING SERVICES DIRECTOR
Brenda Gallmeyer

MANAGING EDITOR Brooke Smith

GRAPHIC DESIGNER Nick Pierce

COPY SUPERVISOR Deborah Morgan

COPY EDITORS Emily Carter, Rebecca Detwiler

TECHNICAL EDITOR Corene Painter

PHOTOGRAPHY SUPERVISOR Tammy Christian

PHOTO STYLISTS Tammy Liechty, Tammy Steiner

PHOTOGRAPHY Matthew Owen

PRODUCTION ARTIST SUPERVISOR
Erin Brandt

PRODUCTION ARTIST Nicole Gage

PRODUCTION ASSISTANSTS Marj Morgan,
Judy Neuenschwander

ISBN: 978-1-59635-393-0
Printed in USA
2 3 4 5 6 7 8 9

Annie's

Exquisite Embellishments for Paper Crafts is published by Annie's, 306 East Parr Road, Berne, IN 46711. Printed in USA. Copyright © 2012, 2013 Annie's. All rights reserved. This publication may not be reproduced in part or in whole without written permission from the publisher.

RETAIL STORES: If you would like to carry this pattern book or any other Annie's publication, visit AnniesWSL.com.

Every effort has been made to ensure that the instructions in this pattern book are complete and accurate. We cannot, however, take responsibility for human error, typographical mistakes or variations in individual work. Please visit AnniesCustomerCare.com to check for pattern updates.

Buyer's Guide

3M
(888) 364-3577
www.3m.com

Art Institute Glitter Inc.
(877) 909-0805
www.artglitter.com

BasicGrey
(801) 544-1116
www.basicgrey.com

Bazzill Basics Paper Inc.
(800) 560-1610
www.bazzillbasics.com

Beacon Adhesives Inc.
(914) 699-3405
www.beaconcreates.com

Bo-Bunny Press
(801) 771-4010
www.bobunny.com

The Cat's Pajamas
http://thecatspajamasrs.com

Clearsnap Inc.
(800) 448-4862
www.clearsnap.com

Cosmo Cricket
(904) 482-0091
http://cosmocricket.com

Crate Paper Inc.
(801) 798-8996
www.cratepaper.com

Darice Inc.
(866) 432-7423
www.darice.com

Darkroom Door
www.darkroomdoor.com

EK Success
www.eksuccessbrands.com

Elizabeth Craft Designs
(805) 485-1529
www.ecraftdesigns.com

Fiskars
(866) 348-5661
www.fiskarscrafts.com

Gina K. Designs
(608) 838-3258
www.ginakdesigns.com

GlueArts
(866) 889-4583
www.gluearts.com

Glue Dots
(888) 458-3368
www.gluedots.com

The Graphics Fairy
http://graphicsfairy.blogspot.com/

Helmar
www.helmarusa.com

Hero Arts
(800) 822-HERO (822-4376)
www.heroarts.com

Imagine Crafts/Tsukineko
(425) 883-7733
www.imaginecrafts.com

Imagination International Inc.
(541) 684-0013
www.copicmarker.com

The Japanese Paper Place
(416) 538-9669
www.japanesepaperplace.com

Jenni Bowlin Studio
www.jbsmercantile.com

Jillibean Soup
(888) 212-1177
www.jillibean-soup.com

Jo-Ann Stores Inc.
(888) 739-4120
www.joann.com

JustRite
(866) 405-6414
www.justritestampers.com

K&Company
www.kandcompany.com

Kaisercraft
(888) 684-7147
www.kaisercraft.net

Krylon
(800) 4KRYLON (457-9566)
www.krylon.com

Layers of Color
www.layersofcolor.com

Lil' Inker Designs
www.lilinkerdesigns.com

Little Yellow Bicycle
(860) 286-0244
www.mylyb.com

Making Memories
(800) 286-5263
www.makingmemories.com

Martha Stewart Crafts
www.eksuccessbrands.com/
marthastewartcrafts

May Arts
(203) 637-8366
www.mayarts.com

Maya Road
(877) 427-7764
www.mayaroad.net

Melissa Frances
(877) 885-1261
www.melissafrances.com

Michaels Stores Inc.
(800) MICHAELS (642-4235)
www.michaels.com

My Favorite Things
www.mftstamps.com

My Mind's Eye
(800) 665-5116
www.mymindseye.com

October Afternoon
(866) 513-5553
www.octoberafternoon.com

Paper and More!
www.paperandmore.com

Papertrey Ink
www.papertreyink.com

Pink Paislee
(816) 883-8259
www.pinkpaislee.com

Plaid Enterprises Inc.
(800) 842-4197
www.plaidonline.com

Prima Marketing Inc.
(909) 627-5532
www.primamarketinginc.com

Provo Craft
(800) 937-7686
www.provocraft.com

Queen & Co.
(858) 613-7858
www.queenandco.com

Ranger Industries Inc.
(732) 389-3535
www.rangerink.com

Really Reasonable Ribbon
www.reasonableribbon.com

Red Lead Paperworks
(314) 962-0433
www.redleadpaperworks.com

Scor-Pal Products
(877) 629-9908
www.scor-pal.com

SCRAPBOOK ADHESIVES BY 3L™
(847) 808-1140
www.scrapbook-adhesives.com

ShinHan USA Inc.
www.shinhanart.co.kr

Simple Stories
(801) 737-3242
http://simplestories.typepad.com

Sizzix
(877) 355-4766
www.sizzix.com

Spellbinders™ Paper Arts
(888) 547-0400
www.spellbinderspaperarts.com

SRM Press Inc.
(800) 323-9589
www.srmpress.com

Stampin' Up!
(800) 782-6787
www.stampinup.com

Sweet 'n Sassy Stamps
(717) 202-5496
www.sweetnsassystamps.com

Therm O Web Inc.
(800) 323-0799
www.thermowebonline.com

Tombow USA
www.tombowusa.com

The Twinery
http://thetwinery.com/

United Notions/Moda Fabrics
(800) 527-9447
www.unitednotions.com

Unity Stamp Co.
(877) 862-2329
www.unitystampco.com

Verve Stamps
http://shopverve.com

Want2Scrap
(260) 740-2976
www.want2scrap.com

We R Memory Keepers
(877) PICKWER (742-5937)
www.weronthenet.com

Webster's Pages
(800) 543-6104
www.websterspages.com

Zva Creative
(801) 243-9281
www.zvacreative.com

The Buyer's Guide listings are provided as a service to our readers and should not be considered an endorsement from this publication.